On Being Ridiculous
— The Power of Laughter in Philosophy and Art

Anders Kølle
in conversation with images by Ashley YK Yeo

First published 2024
All rights reserved

ISBN 978-981-18-8325-5

Cover and Layout Sarah and Schooling
Font FreightNeo Pro

Contents

Introduction

There is nothing funny to say about laughter. To take laughter seriously as an object for thinking one must necessarily kill it. Although people who laugh are, in a sense, touched by great beauty, even wisdom, it is a beauty and wisdom beyond discourse, beyond words. It is a beauty and wisdom that has already found its language: laughter. And so nothing funny has ever been written about laughter. Bergson´s book on the subject is painstakingly dry and Freud´s analysis of the joke is one of the least humorous works imaginable. Laughter is a rare song and to find it one must silence it and lose it. What is lost in terms of good and genuine laughs, however, may be gained in regards to thinking. Laughter is worth thinking about because it presents us with a different image of ourselves and it presents thinking with a different mode and meaning of thinking itself: laughter is thinking turned corporeal, it is thinking with the entire body, thinking from hair roots to toenails. Laughter uses every human cell as its instrument and brings mind and matter, spirit and nature, into a rare, tremoring unison. The link Descartes had such difficulties establishing he would have found had he laughed.

We all have our own, distinct way of laughing. No two people laugh in the exact same way. Something very personal, even private, surfaces and irrupts when we laugh. Laughter exposes us, it renders us vulnerable, it speaks a truth about us that we are not necessarily happy to see revealed. But the force of laughter is too great. It overtakes us. It carries us upwards and outwards, turns all depths into surface, into sound. It is a spasm that renders us wholly visible. Whenever we laugh, we are subjected to this visibility. Herein lies both the source to much embarrassment but also the source to great pleasure: When I laugh I surrender to my own truth. I step into the open with a grin. It is the liberation of a truth that can no longer be tamed, that must burst through: My ugliness and my beauty painted in the air.

Laughter can be used as a weapon. Laughter can be subversive and destructive. To make fun of something or someone is to violently undress them. Weaknesses are magnified, hidden sides are forcefully exposed. Ridicule is called forth to capture and engulf the entirety of a being. It seeps into every movement, every thought, action, and word until the victim of ridicule can do nothing that is not ridiculous. Our shared, human absurdity is projected unto a single being who must now carry the weight of this absurdity on his own. With laughter the one is sacrificed for the many. The many distance themselves. With laughter they create a separate and opposed community cleansed of the absurd. The class clown is loved because he makes this sacrifice voluntarily. He takes the absurdity of everyone upon himself. For this everyone owes him. He expects to be repaid in affection and gratitude. He knows he deserves it.

Laughter is contagious. It spreads through a family, an audience, a public like a virus. It connects across genders and generations. It equalizes high and low, it short-circuits social differences and flattens social hierarchies. It brings the worker and the foreman into a moment´s scattering unison. For this reason laughter has always been feared by people in power. They know and understand by intuition that laughter has the force to question and destabilize power-structures and to expose authorities as ridiculous, as absurd, as unfounded. Humor is incompatible with power. It communalizes what has been culturally and artificially separated, it connects and universalizes the uncommon. Something is shared in laughter that people in power cannot allow to be shared. The contingent, absurd structures that separate men are an absurdity that

Anders Kølle
in conversation with images by Ashley YK Yeo

laughter annihilates in the name of a greater absurdity
that is shared and shareable by all. Hence the total
abolition of humor in most, if not all, dictatorial states
and the limitations and containment of humor that
characterize more liberal state as well. Like sinful smokers
the men and women looking for a good laugh are directed
towards certain pre-defined and well-defined zones of
humor: the Hollywood comedy, the comic strip, the
stand-up show.

What a shame Karl Marx was not a great humorist! What
a pity he chose a specter instead of a clown to carry the
communist message forward.

Laughter is communication. It is a song without words; it is
a melody as old as humanity itself. But what does laughter
"say"? What is its content, its message? Is laughter
a language that can be subjected to semantics and
semiotics? Is there anything to understand in laughter?
Or is laughter, perhaps, a language before all languages,
a language that supersedes every spoken word, every
naming and differentiation? In a sense, then, an original,
Adamic language, like the one Benjamin was looking for,
where all distances between names and things, between
signifiers and signifieds, have yet to manifest themselves?
Why not, at least as a thought-experiment, entertain the
possibility that laughter is humanity´s first articulation
of inarticulate nature – our primordial flirtations with
rhythm and air, with voicing and breathing? If so, laughter
would have to be placed on a threshold – the threshold
between animal voice and human speech, the border
both separating and linking humanity to nature and to the
animal kingdom. To laugh would then mean a return: to
sing with the bird, to growl with the walrus and to howl
both with and against humanity.

Origins without Origin

Etymologically speaking "laughter" resides on an abyss.
It has no Latin or Greek origins to enlighten and explain
the word. The furthest back it can be traced is to the
Old English word "hliehhan" which, in all likelihood,
is onomatopoeic – that is: the word is pure mimicry
and based on nothing but the sound of laughter itself.
The word thus has no semantic history to offer, no
explanatory treasures to be found at the end of a long
line of cultural exchanges and linguistic adaptations. But
in a sense this very lack of explanation, this seeming
emptiness at the very heart of the word might still have
something to tell us. If onomatopoeias are mimicry,
nothing but sound imitation, then onomatopoeias are
no longer words in any conventional sense that signify
by conventional means. Instead of referring to an object
outside themselves, what they are and what they say are
one and the same thing. Sound and meaning become
inseparable as what is meant is nothing but the sound
itself. Onomatopoeias hence play an unusual role in
language and must be situated at the limits and outskirts
of ordinary signification – in a place where language
seems to conflate and fall back on itself to become pure
articulation and sound. The "buzz" of the bee and the
"roar" of the bear are such liminal cases. In imitating
nature, onomatopoeias also imitate and incarnate
the inarticulate voice that is nature´s and bring these
animal voices across the threshold, into human language
where they must necessarily be received as strange
and unsettling guests. Meaning and meaninglessness,
language and non-language, are brought "face to face"
as the bee starts to "buzz" inside the bottle of human
speech. Something is thereby revealed which goes
beyond onomatopoeias and may have importance for a
study of laughter as well: articulate speech is only one
in a myriad of ways in which voices are raised all around
us. Our precious words, ours islands of "logos", are

surrounded to all sides by wordless communication –
which is to say: language is not only world-disclosing it
is also a closure and a limit. In its own way, laughter too
speaks to this limit and never gets tired of crossing it.
In laughter as in onomatopoeias something strange is
brought into language which it can neither absorb nor
fully reject: A Trojan horse of giggles and chuckles rolled
into the House of Being.

From the perspective of language laughter is meaningless
sound. It is the rising and falling of voices without
purpose, signification or intent. Laughter is ridiculous,
laughter is laughable – an absurd transgression of
intelligible speech. Logos and laughter are thus deemed
mutually exclusive and pitched against each other as
adversaries, if not direct enemies: intelligence speaks,
stupidity laughs – the uneducated masses crave laughter
while the educated and enlightened crave writing and
speech. Laughter is thus everywhere expelled from the
Garden of Logos and condemned to a shadowy and
restless wandering. Wherever logos rules, laughter can
be certain to be chased away. But why, we may ask,
this hostility towards laughter? Wherein consists its
transgressions, its crimes? What is it about laughter that
necessitates logos´ forceful rejections?

Perhaps, the problem is not that laughter lies too far
from language but that it lies uncomfortably close. A
firm border is thus deemed necessary to separate the
two. If language were to even partially recognize itself
in laughter it would have to face the limits of its own
powers that laughter so blatantly expose. Far from being
an expression of stupidity or absence of intelligence
and thought, laughter "speaks" its own wisdom and
carries its own truth. But this wisdom and truth always
aims at an expanded field of communication in which

ordinary signification has trouble following suit. Like music laughter puts sound to realms and registers beyond verbalization. Like painting and sculpture it draws lines that exceed the borders of logos´ structured and controllable domains. Laughter is dangerous because every time it breaks through, every time it spins its strange threads in the air, something is brought to the fore that language and logos prefer to forget: human speech and human reason only master pieces of our material and multifaceted world. Concepts only cover caps and coats of the reality in which we live. The distance between sign and object, between language and world that is the very emblem of rational thought is quickly reduced to nothing once the outskirts of logos is reached. Laughter looks back at this border with a grin. Laughter means an acceptance of the unspeakable beyond. Unlike logos laughter is not distance but proximity – sign and world, mind and matter, meaning and meaninglessness brought together in a moment´s embrace. In laughter the flesh "speaks" in all its sensuous, non-conceptual being. In laughter the Real pulls and shakes voices and rings in vocal cords. It moves through the entire body as an earthquake, inscribing its zig-zag fault lines all over trembling bodies and faces. Laughter thus marks a passage that is both an opening and an impasse – a passage passable only to the degree that the mastery of logos and language is left behind. The omnipotence of human speech is the toll that laughter is required to pay. What is won, however, is a jittery step into an expanded field of communication and being and a glimpse of our vast, inhuman beyond.

The conflict between laughter and language stems, however, not only from laughter´s transgressions but also from laughter´s tendency to generalize what language is very careful to separate and keep apart. The

Anders Kølle
in conversation with images by Ashley YK Yeo

fine-meshed nets of differentiations by which language
seeks to capture the world are nets that get tangled and
entwined in laughter that knows not how to use such fine
and delicate nets. But this inability to differentiate is also
what gives laughter its unique ability to gather and unite.
In laughter, people otherwise separated by cultural and
national borders are offered a shared and common voice.
For a moment, however brief, one tongue of laughter
replaces the many tongues of speech. Laughter has a
special affinity with the common and is evoked only where
some sort of communality can be found. What is funny
is always something shared, something that "speaks"
to the common absurdity of our human condition: the
man who trips and falls is not funny because he falls but
because of the strangeness in walking upright that his fall
briefly illuminates and reveals; the man who sweats and
stammers when declaring his love is not funny because
he sweats and stammers but because of the absurdity
that lies at the heart of all human love. There is, in other
words, only laughter where there is recognition and only
recognition where something we have already thought
and already felt is presented to us anew. Hence both the
honesty but also the embarrassment that follows laughter
like a shadow: to laugh means to take the truth of the
absurd upon oneself – to declare: I too am grotesque. I
know the human absurdity well.

If *being* means *being absurd* it is because being overflows
logos in all directions. What logos and language can no
longer follow and contain is summoned by the word
"absurd". "Absurd" therefore describes nothing but a limit
– a poor attempt on the side of logos to speak what can
no longer be said. That the absurd is much vaster, much
richer and deeper, than language is able to express is,
however, constantly confirmed and expressed in laughter.
The rising and falling of laughing voices, the ringing and

circles made in the air, are only absurd to the degree logos is able to convince us that nothing of human interest and value is expressed thereby. To develop an ear for laughter is to move in the opposite direction – to explore the heights and depths, the voices and registers beyond logos. Comedians must develop such an ear and become explorers of such worlds. Comedians professionalize in giggling journeys into the depths of logos´ beyond. Their journeys are often characterized by some element of physicality, some encounter with bodies and matter, since our bodily being, our naked presence is precisely where language with its concepts and distances, its separations and differentiations is sure to break down. If much humor takes a seemingly vulgar path to reach this point it is not for the sake of vulgarity itself but because vulgarity and the reality of our bare, human existence in important ways coincide. Drives and functions beyond our control "speak" of these incomprehensible realms. The flesh is an unending mystery, a source of never ending wonder and marvel. A single look in the mirror suffices to show just how little logos captures and understands. Only by habit and blindness is it possible to live these odd bodies of ours without succumbing to constant amazement. In this sense humor is easy: the strangeness and ridiculousness of being is never far away – it is enough to show us what we already know to provoke laughter. The good jokes are already there – in the present of a presence that remains unspeakable and unfathomable to the human mind.

When signification collapses in humor, when reason is driven beyond reason, language is faced with beginnings as well as with closures and ends. Somehow language must have originated from the speechless nature surrounding it; somehow it must have abstracted its first words and sentences from the "absurd" beyond. In the beginning was not the Word but inarticulate matter.

Anders Kølle
in conversation with images by Ashley YK Yeo

This is the dirty joke whispered by nature. The ability
to form distant and distancing signs, the human gift of
representation, is only conceivable as the end point of a
long journey through inarticulate presence and matter.
However thoroughly language tries to separate itself
from this fact, dirt stains of the "absurd" still blemish the
House of Being. To give an example: When Wittgenstein
uses the concept of games to show how words and
sentences mean, he brings not only rules and order
but also contingency and disorder across the doorstep
to language. If the meaning of words is not stable but
depends on the language game being played then surely
the words themselves are meaningless and "absurd"
outside the games in which they are used. Or to put it
another way: If language plays chess in the morning and
bridge in the afternoon, if it plays tennis on weekends and
cricket during the week, then surely the rules of language
are themselves ruled by something unspeakable and
"absurd". The ridiculous seeps into the rules of language
that can no longer secure themselves from strange and
illogical foundations. Meaning rests on meaningless
laws as nonsensical as senseless nature. Inadvertently
Wittgenstein´s language philosophy is thus touched by
something bizarre, if not comical, that comes very close
to the illogical logic of Humpty Dumpty: "When I use a
word... it means just what I choose it to mean – neither
more nor less." It is a tightrope walk: If a word means
more than it means it does not mean, if it means less
than it means it does not mean either, and if it means just
what it means then it does, indeed, mean but the meaning
itself is absurd. What Lewis Carroll approaches from
the side of humorous nonsensical sense, Wittgenstein
addresses through serious sensical nonsense. The result
is very similar: Language must give way to absolute
strangeness in its midst. Bizarre characters raise their
threshold voices. Laughter irrupts precisely where Carroll

seeks it and where Wittgenstein finds it without wanting it. The outside of language is already inside and words are already tainted by meaningless, sticky matters. Like Humpty Dumpty language resembles an egg that reflects poorly on its own origins. But what came first: laughter or language? Nonsense or sense? The answer sits on the top of a wall, surrounded by meaningless nature.

Turn-of-Breath

Laughter is a turn-of-breath – it is a different speed and rhythm of respiration, it is a new sounding and voicing of air: air snapped in chuckling lumps from speechless, shimmering surfaces. At times laughter´s turning of breath turns into an out of breath, into a lack of breath, when laughter uses too much air too quickly. Unlike speech laughter is a big spender of air. It does not know how to moderate its expenses. It breathes as if the world was nothing but air, as if everything around it was pure generosity and giving.

The German word for a turn-of-breath is "Atemwende". The term has come to play an important role in an area that, at least to begin with, would appear very foreign to laughter, namely in the solemn field of poetic writing. It is Paul Celan who first gave "Atemwende" its poetic significance when he introduced the term in his famous Meridian Speech in the following way: "Literature: that can signify a turn-of-breath. Who knows, perhaps literature travels its path – which is also the path of art – for the sake of such a breath turning?… perhaps it succeeds here in distinguishing between strangeness and strangeness, perhaps at precisely this point the Medusa´s head shrivels, perhaps the robots cease to function – for this unique, fleeting moment? Is perhaps at this point, along with the I – with the estranged I, set free *at this point* and *in a similar manner* – is perhaps at this point an Other set free?"[1]

It is curious and thought-provoking that what Celan is describing here should be poetry, not laughter. Surely, the similarities between the two are striking: What, we may ask, is laughter but a place where strangeness is present and where an estranged I is set free? What is laughter but a fleeting moment, where something shrivels, comes out of order, stops to function, to let

[1] Jacques Derrida, *Sovereignties in Question – The Poetics of Paul Celan* (New York: Fordham University Press, 2005), p. 180

an Other emerge? And this emergence made possible through a breach in speech, through a turning of breath, an "Atemwende"! If this is poetry rather than laughter, if this is art rather than humor, then it must be a laughable and humorous art. It must be an art that liberates the I through means indistinguishable from those adopted and applied by laughter. Yet, there is no record of Celan having laughed during his Meridian Speech nor of an audience succumbing to uncontrollable giggles and tee-hee. Is poetry too serious to acknowledge its own laughable affinities? Or is Celan, perhaps, attempting to do something else, namely to approach what is serious in laughter, poetic in ridicule instead of the other way around? If, as Celan says, the path traveled by literature – which is also the path of art – is chosen for the sake of a breath turning, then the "Atemwende" of laughter might have some poetic and artistic value as well. Art and laughter would then be close relatives and travel companions in the beyond of ordinary writing and speech.

If poetry is in search of a different breath to liberate the strange from the grips of logos and language then poetry is truly in the pursuit of something odd: with the use of language, language must be transgressed, with the use of words, words must be overcome – in order to say the unsayable poetry must "speak". Poetry appears, thus, to be trapped in a terrible self-contradiction: what it needs in order to escape is the very thing it is running from. Language is both poetry´s vehicle and cage, its escape-route and its limitation. If only poetry could be poetry without speaking, without words, then, one should think, poetry would be better off. Celan himself seems to confirm as much: "To be sure, there can be no doubt that the poem – the poem today – shows a strong inclination toward falling silent. And this, I believe, has only an indirect relationship to the difficulties of word

² Ibid., p. 181

selection... the poem takes its position at the edge of itself; in order to be able to exist, it without interruption calls and fetches itself from its now-no-longer back into its as-always."² If complete silence is tempting it is because silence would fulfill poetry´s greatest desires without detours, without more hard work and further complications. Silence would immediately save poetry from itself. And yet, such a rescue is not possible but must remain a dream, a poetic "inclination": where there is no longer any limits to be crossed there is also no longer any "estranged I" in need of rescue. To be a trespasser and a liberator poetry needs borders as well as prisons. Hence poetry must constantly oscillate back and forth between words, it must move away from language in order to come back to language and it must come back in order to move away. Poetry takes its position "at the edge of itself" – that is: in a place that is not so much a place as a non-place, an utopia, and in a position that describes less a position than a constant movement.

But as serious as these thoughts and this analysis surely are, who can deny that they are also, at least, slightly ridiculous – that there is, following Celan, something quite absurd at work in the poetic work itself? Celan – although not known for his great jokes and his sparkling sense of humor – does show a clear affinity with the absurd – something which he does not deny but both acknowledges and embraces in several places in the Meridian Speech. Most important in this regard is, perhaps, the figure of the "Kunstblinde" woman, Lucile – a literary figure who is blind to art and who therefore perceives art and all talk of art in a different and seemingly silly, seemingly idiotic, way. Celan describes the "Kunstblinde" Lucile thus: "But when art is being talked about there is always someone present who doesn´t listen very carefully. More precisely: someone who hears

³ Ibid., p. 174

and listens and looks... and then doesn´t know what the conversation was all about. But who hears the speaker, who "sees him speak", who has perceived language and form, and at the same time – what doubt could there be in the world of this drama? – at the same time has perceived breath, that is, direction and fate. This person is – as you have guessed... Lucile."³ The "Kunstblinde" Lucile, the woman who is blind to art, is, before anything else, "blind" to language – or rather: she is blind to a particular perception of language. She does not know how to distance herself. She is too close: too close to the breath of language, too close to its form and its palpable, material being. Instead of listening she hears, instead of hearing she sees, instead of seeing she looks. She is constantly caught on the wrong "level" and therefore does not know, when the conversation ends, "what the conversation was all about". But what is the "right level", the "right" distance to language? It seems, following Celan, that poetry does not know the answer to this question either and that poetry itself is therefore, in this very sense, as lost and even as "Kunstblinde" as Lucile. But if this blindness means losing the content of speech it also and at the same time means to gain access to something else: only to the one who does not really listen or who seems to be focusing and listening to the wrong things does language reveal its breathing and rhythmical side – only to the one who is semantically "out of tune" can language become tune, tone and music. The poem takes, as Celan says, its position at the edge of itself. But does this also mean that the "Kunstblinde" – the one who is blind to art – is the only true poet and artist? A grotesque and laughable proposition! Yet, is this not precisely what Celan suggests?

If laughter, as previously put forward, is the child of lost or confused distances between sign and matter, between meaning and nonsense, then poetry, in the interpretation offered here, is born out of very similar circumstances. And like laughter, what poetry gains from this very loss and confusion is the ability to "speak" inside a larger field of communication and to address what lies beyond the borders and limits of logos. In poetry as in laughter something foreign is thereby set free, something strange is emancipated. The flow of being that overflows logos in all directions is followed across the thresholds of meaning and into territories unspeakable and invisible to common sense. The "Kunstblinde" is, in other words, a seer, and what she sees must make her laugh. Poetry and laughter share an impulse and share a knowledge that needs new and different voices to be sung. The giggles and roars of laughter and the rhythms of line and verse are witnesses to the same "absurd". Only the blindness of logos can prevent such recognition – or as Celan says: "Can we now, perhaps, find the place where strangeness was present, the place where a person succeeded in setting himself free, as an – estranged – I? Can we find such a place, such a step?"[4] Yes, we do find it. And we find it in more places than one.

[4] Ibid., p. 179

Silly Art

It must be the result of a great fear of the unspeakable that more art is not found funny. Why else do we hear so little laughter in museums and galleries when so much of what is presented is profoundly silly? Too much language, too much logos and too little "Kunstblinde" governs the day. Art is smothered in speech and in writing and strangled in meaning and discourse. Everyone who is anyone must have something clever to say. Instead of proximity art is held at a distance and this distance is a protective wall. It protects us from facing the ridiculousness of being and it saves us from rescuing our strange and mysterious I´s. One misses the Humpty Dumpty on top of this wall with all the risks of falling so richly and abundantly present. One misses his nonsensical sense and his sensical nonsense when he presents the abyss in meaning and speech. In art too, we have an egg laid by a most mysterious and laughable hen. But this hen is slaughtered and put in the freezer as soon as the egg has been laid. It requires thus a turn-of-breath, an "Atemwende", to save art´s ridiculous world. It requires an entire rewriting of the history of modern art – this time full of flaws and imperfections – and carried out in the name and with the purpose of a strange and liberating laugh.

It is the great tragedy of Marcel Duchamp that so few people found him funny. The artist, who more than anyone, produced laughable things and explained these laughable things with laughable thoughts and ideas was his entire life surrounded by the greatest imaginable solemnity. Indeed it is so obvious that it feels strange to point it out: his *Fountain* is a marvelous joke. It quite literally takes the piss out of the art world by bringing the piss – or its destination – inside. It is a joke so far from being subtle, so far from any refinement that it was immediately turned both subtle and refined. One

must, so to speak, turn a deaf ear to this cultivation and
sophistication to give some laughter back to the joke.
One must become a "Kunstblinde" to see how laughter
and art connects. The beasts that Duchamp carried into
the museums are still calling to be set free.

What does it mean to be blind to art when confronted
with Duchamp´s urinal? It first of all means not to see the
urinal as art but as a urinal. And then it might mean not
even to see the urinal as a urinal but as a rather ridiculous
object created for the purpose of a rather ridiculous
thing. Before there are urinals there are human beings
with basic physical needs. This is the hen of this porcelain
egg. To be truly blind to art would thus mean to allow
both the urinal and its users to be what they really are:
absurd. Where the fountain begins to spurt is also where
human pride and self-importance recede and make way
for the strange and laughable existence that is ours (and
now I am trying to explain the joke and the joke is no
longer funny. Please, forgive me for taking laughter and
art too seriously!)

The *Fountain* is not speech but matter – it is not a sign
but a presence. Duchamp did not represent a urinal but he
placed the thing itself before us. If nothing else matters,
this surely does since this very presence is precisely
what language with all its distances and differentiations
has such a hard time to capture and logos such a hard
time trying to understand. The *Fountain* is too close, not
enough sign, not enough signifying and signification but
stupidly and meaninglessly there. It is in every aspect
a dumb thing – nothing but piss flows through it. But
discourse is capable of its own "Atemwende", logos can
perform its own turn of breath. If stupidity is turned
into brilliance, if strangeness and silliness is turned into
art, perhaps, even great art, then the embarrassment of

language and logos in front of this absurd, immoveable
presence is magically gone. Language can return to
its usual operations, logos return to its traditional
self-importance and pride – or, as Celan would put it:
the robots and the Medusa´s head are working again.
Meanings and distances are thus invented which are
nothing but constructions and make-belief. The experts,
the art historians, can write new chapters for new books
and the museum guides find that there is, once again,
plenty to say. Language and logos win. The threat posed
by the strange and the silly has been eliminated. Presence
is once more presentable, representable and meaningful.
If the prize to be paid is the odd and unlikely elevation
of a urinal into the highest spheres of art, then so be it.
Rather have piss at the top of the art world than risk the
embarrassment of having nothing to say.

What might appear as a unique example provoking an
unusual response is, in fact, neither. Throughout the 20th
century, language and logos have been called numerous
times to perform and repeat this maneuver – each time to
a similar effect. One needs only think of what happened
to the nonsense and subversive humor and poetry of
Dada to find a similar case. The tragedy of the avant-
garde is not only, as Peter Bürger has famously stated,
that art never managed to break down the institutional
walls separating art from life, but also and no less
importantly that art did not manage to keep its roaring
laughter in front of logos – that art, in effect, did not
keep and preserve its "Kunstblinde".

The trophies hung on the walls of logos have since then
multiplied and ranges from Samuel Beckett in one end to
Andy Warhol in the other. Who, for example, would not
admit that there is something profoundly silly at work in
Warhol´s series of Campbell´s Soup Cans – something

much too silly and laughable to be reduced to serious writing and speech? And are not Kafka, Joyce, and Beckett writers who write tragic comedies and comic tragedies about the absurd rules that rule language itself – and, by consequence, human reason: the unreasonable reasonability that founds nothing but an abyss? Are they not the Wittgensteins and Humpty Dumptys of literature balancing on signification´s outer edge? And what if not some strange perversion can turn John Cage´s symphonic silences into something that is not ridiculous and laughable but demands the greatest attention and respect? If so, are we not listening and seeing in the wrong way? Are we not perpetually too far away and thus hearing and seeing too much art? Should we not learn from Celan´s Lucile and move closer instead – that is: lose art in order to find it, respect art enough to allow it to be silly and absurd? If this sounds paradoxical it is because it does suggest to leave all meaning, all "doxa", behind in order to catch a brief glimpse of the realities outside reason that art and laughter approach hand in hand. It is a leap, it is an "Atemwende", it is a strange hen brought back to life. It is also the point where stammering, inarticulate voices – the voices of both laughter and art – bear witness to the ridiculousness of logos itself: the unfounded foundation that is so fearful of good and genuine laughs.

Surely, the victories of language and logos are never so final and convincing that they rest forever safe from hesitation and doubt. It takes, for example, a very cool art historian not to fumble and blush just a little in front of Duchamp´s mustached *Mona Lisa* "with a hot ass". Laughter has a remarkable ability to return and rattle the cages of speech. Every time art is being described and talked about something quite stupid and ridiculous threatens to slip back in. In fact, one would be hard pressed to think of just a single theory of art that steers completely free of the absurd. Art forces great men and women to make strange formulations and silly calls. Are we sure, for example, that we know what a "disinterested pleasure" is – and that if, should such a pleasure really exist, it would not be something both paradoxical and absurd? Or can we say with true conviction that art understood as "purposiveness without purpose" is not a weird self-contradiction that – with or without purpose – brings something unspeakable and unthinkable in? Is it, in other words, not only the sternness of our books and the solemnity of our teachers that prevent us from giggling and chuckling in the classroom´s back? How logos must be bended and twisted to talk about art! How meaning must become meaningless to state something meaningful! One must imagine Kant on top of one of his countless philosophical walls proclaiming, in all seriousness: "When I use a word it means just what I choose it to mean – nothing more nor less." One will, thus, have to take Kant on his word: "Yes, pleasure does not need to be interested. Such a thing as disinterested pleasure truly exists. Yes, purposiveness without purpose is, indeed, thinkable. I am pretty sure, I have encountered it in art." But is this not the robots and the Medusa´s head that now return to haunt us? And would not at least a giggle be called for and justified? Why not embrace our inner Lucile – the one "who hears and listens and looks... and then doesn´t know what the conversation was all about."[5]

One will have to be a fan of walls to be a fan of serious art theory. And one will have to keep erecting them since they constantly crumble and fall. The artificial separation of laughter and art that is so important to this solemn branch of thinking is always in need of repairs and re-enforcements. There is always someone who does not really understand and who needs to be escorted

[5] Ibid., p. 174

⁶ See: https://
www.theartstory.
org/movement/
situationist-
international/

down the wall. To provide an example of such hopeless stupidity: What is the difference between a Dada poetry reading and a Monty Python sketch? Or what is the difference between a Situationist intervention and candid camera? Or, to be even more seriously ridiculous: wherein lies the difference between a dead parrot that does not speak and a pianist who does not play? To every true art historian and art theorist the difference is strikingly obvious. So obvious that it never occurs to them to even ask. To others, the imbeciles and the Luciles of this world, the difference is less striking. They might, even, have difficulties separating the two at all: For didn´t Dada make them laugh? And didn´t Monty Python make them think? Surely, such confused souls might then read up on the subject and learn something like: "the Situationist International was a radical movement devoted to the disruption and reimagining of the systems which govern everyday life."[6] These are impressive words. It is hard not to be impressed. And since nothing as impressive has ever been said or written about Monty Python the difference should now be obvious to all. But is it? The "Kunstblinde" are hard to get rid of. They are guests who exceed their welcome and show no signs of leaving anytime soon. For example: Are concepts enough to save art from ridicule? And isn´t it then a sad kind of art that is saved – an art that is brought into separate and separating discourse instead of uniting in a roaring laugh?

Thinking with the Body

Laughter comes in many shapes and guises: it is a silver-thread that hangs in the air; it is a roaring and growling beast; it is a clicking dolphin that surfaces for a moment before returning to its invisible depths. Everyone has his or her own way of speaking the unspeakable and of approaching language´s beyond. It is done with grace and elegance and it is done noisily, stammering, stumbling. For our strange I´s to be set free strange ways are called for. What summons and unites us in laughter everyone must seek out in his own manner and style. Our shared absurdity is shareable because all of us must live it individually, incarnate it by ourselves. Surely, this is part of the absurdity: so many trembling bodies and faces to express a human condition that remains everywhere the same.

What Heidegger and Merleau-Ponty sought through years of work and writing, laughter brings about in a second: laughter places us in the world. No tours or detours through philosophy are needed when thinking and matter come together in laughs. The mind cannot ignore its carnal existence but lands in the middle of being with a splash. In a very palpable, physical way, then, laughter entails a short-cut through everything that Western culture has done so much to distance and keep apart: spirit versus matter, thinking versus object, God versus world. Indeed, the concept of culture itself is founded on an opposition that laughter questions in its own noisy and demolishing way: nature and animals are brought dangerously close to the human border and come to question and threaten the very exclusivity of man. The threshold between human and inhuman is never so obvious that it is not obviously crossable at numerous points.

It was the "dogs" among the Ancient Greeks, the Cynics, who with the greatest effects explored the frailties and weaknesses of the proud and isolated figure of man.

Anders Kølle
in conversation with images by Ashley YK Yeo

To mention just one famous example: When Plato was
appraised for his definition of man as a featherless biped,
Diogenes the Cynic plucked the feathers from a cock,
brought it to Plato´s school, and said: "Here is Plato´s
man." This attack on the thinker of the loftiest and purest
Ideas – the man who tolerated no smudged fingers
grasping for the Good, the True, and the Beautiful – is
significant for several reasons: not only did it ridicule
the very idea of man as an idea, separable from the
rest of the animal kingdom, but it did so by doing what
humor does best: by substituting differentiation with
communality. Or, more precisely: Diogenes act is not only
funny because man and rooster are so obviously different
but also, and more importantly, because in several crucial
aspects they are not. For a moment – however brief –
man must look at the rooster and the rooster must look
back at man and something shared is brought to the fore.
Man and rooster are but two different "formulations"
of the same unspeakable and unfathomable truth. They
equally participate in the grand and absurd mystery
that is life. By projecting the image of the rooster unto
man all sorts of contingencies must surface and soon
beg answers to question of the strangest and queerest
kinds: why a mouth instead of a beak? Why arms and
skin instead of feathers and wings? Why language and
philosophy instead of cock-a-doodle-doos? Diogenes´
rooster is an earthquake in knowledge. It shakes all
convictions and certainties that we may have. It is thus
a kind of thinking that thinks beyond common reason to
explore what thought itself can barely reach. Indeed, it
would be nothing short of the sublime were this concept
not much too proud and self-important to describe what
we are grasping for here – namely the moment when
thinking thinks against the certainties of knowledge to
set the strangeness of being free.

If laughter is often casted in the role of the silly it is because people in power fear it so. They miss no chance to ostracize it and to diminish it. Laughter is associated with stupidity, with depravity, with mental deprivation. The creative overflow of thinking, the precious connections that laughter establishes and brings to light are thus turned into their opposite: into lack, into darkness, into obscenity. One accepts the "kidders", the "pranksters" only as long as they on their side accept the general "rules of the game" and limit their humor to a few harmless remarks made at the far end of the dinner table. The absurdity of being is silenced: intelligent girls and well-behaved boys keep it in the dimples of an indifferent smile and learn how to "save" the absurd for later: for the annual trip to Disneyland, for late afternoon cartoons and comic books. The Cynical roosters are caged and are allowed their transgressive behavior only within the confines of well-defined programs and formats. After all, comedy is also business and as a business it is understandable, logical, acceptable. Mickey Mouse and Goofy are no longer cynics in the original sense but only in a modern, profitable meaning.

But however thoroughly the absurd is ostracized and repressed it constantly finds new ways back in. Death is an absurdity that is much too real to be limited to pre-defined programs and formats. Sex is an absurdity that constantly wants to be real and is much too desirable to be "saved" for later. In both, the ridiculousness of being returns to question the limits of man – in both, something must be thought that can only be thought in raw, physical terms: like animals we copulate; like animals we die. Sex and death are beginnings and ends in which mind and matter must unite, in which abstract ideas explain nothing. Thought is flesh and flesh is thought and reason can no longer separate these oceans. It is an overflowing, even when death is concerned, because death, like sex, returns us to the absurd foundations of being – the unspeakable beyond that is manifestly here, in our flesh and blood, in our absurd being in the middle of the absurdity of the world: Our here and now completely undressed, unprotected from the contingencies of living.

And in between – when neither sex nor death is there to call thinking into flesh? When there are no roosters, no pranksters, no joke-crackers around? When we are apparently just living our serious, humorless, "meaningful" lives – caught up in the daily "meaningful" decisions of our "meaningful" careers, making "meaningful" plans for our "meaningful" futures? What then? Isn´t the absurd here rendered invisible – hidden behind too many layers of habits, structures, and forced, artificial meanings? Doesn´t the nonsense of this sense make any senseless nonsense impossible? Well, even then one can never rest assured that a laugh will not suddenly irrupt and illuminate what "meaning" keeps hidden. All it takes is a single odd regard to undress our everyday reality to the bones. As in a Kafkaesque story everything before us abruptly changes and takes on mysterious, unusual shapes: families look strange, jobs look strange, ambitions look strange – entire cities and societies look strange. Our here and now calls all projects and projections back to their absurd and inexplicable base. From the point of view of "reason" and power this regard is destructive and subversive. From the perspective of our estranged I´s it is pure liberation: it is the regard that undresses kings and queens, presidents and ministers and makes bosses look remarkably silly. It is the regard that recognizes high and low as members of the same human absurdity. The order of the day, all structures and rules are forced into contingency´s embrace. The distances and differentiations that are the masterpiece of logos, that makes the robots function and the Medusa head turn, is suddenly nothing but air – breathable, laughable air – the air of an "Atemwende" that return all majesties to the majesty of the absurd.

Giggles in the Garden of Eden

There is something very odd and, dare we say, quite ridiculous about the way the first man and woman, Adam and Eve, make their appearance in the Bible. There they are, living happily and peacefully inside God´s grand nudist camp until, after taking a bite of the forbidden fruit, they discover their own nakedness, get terribly red cheeked and embarrassed and soon find themselves expelled from the camp, forever forbidden to return. It is a bad vaudeville act – a sort of mistaken and reversed striptease in which what should have been the end comes at the beginning instead. Adam and Eve realize their nakedness too late or they realize it too soon – it comes down to the same thing since they shouldn´t have realized it at all. Knowledge of good and evil is first and foremost knowledge of being nude, of being corporeal, of being man and woman with everything that this entails. It is a distanced and distancing look in which the body becomes strange and the sex an oddity, a perversion. Strictly speaking, Adam and Eve discover nothing new but only what was already there, what they already are, and therein lies also the entire reason for their shame: they discover that they are absurd – they see that they belong entirely to unreasonable, senseless nature. This is the moment when they could have laughed, when they could have made the whole garden tremble with a liberating roar. Instead they looked at each other and looked at themselves and felt terribly embarrassed. Original sin and the fall of man were thus born in the absence of a laugh and founded on Adam´s and Eve´s regrettable lack of a sense of humor.

Once again, we will return to the concepts of Celan to better understand this peculiar story, although his concepts must now be turned in the opposite direction: not away from logos and discourse but towards them instead. For what is God´s law, the law that Adam

and Eve breaks, if not a law of blindness, a certain
"Sexblinde", that is imposed to protect man from
seeing and witnessing his own absurdity? And what is
the realization of this absurdity but a sudden and painful
"Atemwende" that forcefully exposes Adam and Eve to
the fullness of their own strange and inexplicable being?
We must assume that God had good intentions when
he imposed the law: the absurd is bearable as long as it
is not seen and recognized as such. It is possible to live
happily in the absurd if the absurd is not confronted and
questioned. Indeed, the absurd only becomes properly
and truly "absurd" once a step backwards is taken that
reveals and "undresses" this always already nude reality.
The absurd is, in other words, born the moment it is no
longer lived naively and blindly, the moment it comes to
stand senseless and naked before us. And surely the Bible
is right in making this the decisive step in the history of
man – the step that plunges humanity into a world of
mortality, sickness, and wretchedness – or, what we might
also call: the world of discourse, logos and progress.
Without this step humans would not be humans. They
would still be blind to their nakedness, blind to their
bodily strangeness. They would still live in the eternity of
the naked now of the Garden of Eden. The importance
of this step can, therefore, hardly be overestimated.
All human culture is based on it. And yet, how can we
ignore that this step is also so little: a small retreat, a
little interval, a bit of empty space in front of an awkward
body. It doesn't save man from being absurd and it
doesn't explain man's existence – it does, however, make
this absurdity shameful and this inexplicability feared.

If nature is not full of laughing birds roaming the skies
and mammals walking the savannahs with grinning
faces, if nature seems disappointedly humorless and
dry, it is because the animal, unlike man, does not

have any estranged I in need of rescue and liberation.
The strangeness that the animal is, is only visible from
the distant position of man. In all likelihood, since this
must remain pure speculation, no bird is overwhelmed
with a feeling of absurdity of being a bird and no
mammal shutters in front of its own, senseless being.
Nature seems incapable of reflecting upon itself since
it is incapable of being naked. Without this founding
nakedness, without this lack of a lack, the animal never
comes to question itself or to feel ashamed of its bodily
being. The animal is "Sexblinde" – as God supposedly
intended it – and fully submerged in its own strangeness.
Nothing can make it blush since it has no undressed truth
to cover. Its naked reality is, in other words, not naked
but simply real. But can we conclude from this, as so
many thinkers before us, that the animal doesn´t feel and
doesn´t think? Can we rob it of all abilities and powers?
Is feeling only feeling when it is based on some kind of
shame and thinking only thinking as self-observation? Is
there, in other words, nothing else to feel and nothing
else to think about than nakedness and shame? If this
is what constitutes the poverty of the animal, its being
"poor-in-world", one must fear what it means to be
rich. The House of Being stands erected on a couple of
blushing cheeks and hands reaching in panic for a fig
leaf. The difference that distinguishes and supposedly
dignifies man is a difference founded in trembling flesh.
Animal and man thus stand opposed to each other only as
the result of the peculiar inability of man to accept and
come to terms with his own strangeness, to fully live his
own absurdity. He sees his flesh and he doesn´t want to
see it. He senses his own absurdity and he doesn´t want
to sense it. May we ask: Is language a way of closing our
eyes, and logos a way of numbing our senses? Are they
walls erected to shut our shame out? Surely, new worlds
are constructed within these walls – worlds of science,

worlds of philosophy, worlds of culture – but the panic
of our nudity, of our fundamental strangeness still seem
to haunt these worlds. The fig leaf is never big enough,
there is always some embarrassing part it doesn´t cover.
Scientific revolution follows scientific revolution as
so many hands searching for the perfect leaf: the leaf
that can cover the universe, the leaf that can cover the
human sex. It is the same leaf: to cover the absurd with
a mathematic formula, with a sentence, with an equation
and then to rejoice that the absurd has finally gone away.

The shame of being who we are: how kings and
churches through the centuries have benefitted from
this unshakeable feeling – and how businesses and
corporations continue to benefit today! Entire industries
and economies are based on our self-contempt and on
our blushing cheeks in front of the mirror. No matter
how we dress our bodies, no matter how we veil our
existence and with how many houses and cars we cover
our shameful nakedness something of our Adamic
embarrassment always remains. To cover the absurd
with more absurdities doesn´t free us from the absurd.
There is a crack in every swimming pool, a hole in every
designer dress that always leaves part of us unsatisfied.
And something looks at us through these cracks and
holes that fills us with distress and anguish. The economy
of shame is also an economy of fear. Buying new
things looks a terribly lot like an obsessive compulsive
disorder, set and kept in motion to ward off our fears.
We dress up in layers of useless objects only to find
that the absurd has not gone away. If this doesn´t lead
to anxiety and panic attacks it leads to melancholia and
depression instead. The modern mood or "Stimmung"
seems to leave only these two options open. The only
question is: which one shall it be today? Meanwhile, new
supercomputers are being constructed that once and

for all promises to bypass the age-old problem: here is man´s double but without a feeling of shame, here is man´s shadow finally freed of the troubling flesh. The computer needs no fig leaf – it has never been naked and shall never be so. It is wonderfully free of the attributes that make men and women blush. With the most sophisticated technologies something incredible complex is build that is to solve the most basic and primitive of problems: our shameful, bodily existence. If this sounds implausible, even outrageous, allow us to bring the father of modern computers onto the stand and witness for us: Alan Turing, this marvelous mathematician and engineer, whose homosexuality, however, was such a source of shame and embarrassment that he ended his own life when prosecuted for his "promiscuous" and, at the time, unlawful behavior. And how did he choose to kill himself? By eating a poison-injected apple. Indeed, the original sin is never far away and the birth of computers stands in the most intimate relation to it. Apple computers is a newer branch on the same Biblical tree that blossoms with digital, flesh-bypassing solutions. Shamelessly unashamed they promise a way out of all shame. It is the most high-tech solution to the most low-tech problem. The strangeness, the absurdity of this is, however, clothed in the usual discourse: the computer means progress and looks only ahead. Steve Jobs did a fantastic job in being the cool prophet of unsentimental and unashamed technical solutions. And yet his entire empire was built on the same sweaty forehead that has travelled from Adam and Eve to the technophiles and computer enthusiasts of today.

We have said it before but let us repeat it in this Biblical context: laughter means a return to the absurd conditions that are ours. Laughter is not a fig leaf but this fig leaf momentarily removed. It exposes us to our shame, it confronts us with our nakedness but liberates this shame and this nakedness from its sinful and repressive dimensions. Laughter is always paradisiac in that it embraces instead of rejects the strangeness of our flesh. At the same time, however, laughter is only possible because this strangeness remains strange. As self-reflexive, self-observant beings we are forever barred from the complete annulment of the absurd in which the animal lives. In laughter our nakedness is kept, Adam and Eve stay by our side, but the response to our nakedness is radically different: we do not look at ourselves in horror but with a grin. We are still the ones who have eaten the forbidden fruit, we are still the homeless wanderers of this earth, still the exiles and the damned, but in laughter we take this with surprising lightness. This is not a Nietzschean laughter that comes from on high and dives like an eagle into the hearts of men. There is nothing lofty and elevated about genuine laughter. Its movement is not vertical but horizontal. It remains close to the earth, close to the tree, close to the flesh and close to the inexplicable mystery that is ours.

Dining with Dictators

Royals smile often but rarely laugh. Dictators pout much and rarely even smile. The more power is concentrated the further removed it is from laughs. Laughter and power simply do not get along. The absurdity that laughing lets in, the human vulnerability and uncertainty it exposes is incompatible with power. Power is born serious and it needs to take the world and, not least, itself seriously. Otherwise, one might ask, who would?

If we have already described the ties between laughter and strangeness that turn laughter and power into adversaries, we have yet to examine the very stage or seat of this conflict in its most concrete and palpable dimension. The human mouth is the true battlefield of opposed and opposing forces. It is where both logos and laughter fight for the same space. Power wants to use the mouth for one purpose and laughter wants to use it for another. The mouth is the passage, the organ, the opening that must somehow accommodate both. It is the Suez Canal of these opposing tankers. The schizophrenia of human reality, the split between matter and concept, nature and culture, body and language is concentrated in the mouth that is bound to serve both sides equally: to eat, to drink, to laugh, to speak, to chatter, to reason, to yell, to command. If the ego, according to Freud, has a hard time serving three masters, the mouth, we should think, has it even worse.

Power always entails a disciplining of the mouth. This vulnerable passage between body and world, between inner and outer, must be hardened and fortified through mastery and control. No contingencies, slips of tongue, strange accents or accidental strangeness are allowed. Stuttering, stammering kings are, if lucky, loved for their humanity but must constantly fight for the people´s respect. Too many breaks, too much spit and respiration

calls attention to matter instead of concepts. The silliness
and senselessness of the body steals the scene. We
know that Hitler rehearsed every speech he gave until he
knew each syllable and comma by heart. This very vain
mouth with its vain, little moustache hanging threatening
over it like an eternal exclamation mark was drilled and
disciplined like an elite soldier. Every speech was an attack
and every attack was meticulously planned in advance.
The oratorical brilliance of this man, the rhetoric that
spellbound an entire nation and, eventually, threw the
entire world into war, was not simply a (poisonous) gift
of nature but the result of days and weeks of practice
in front of mirrors, cameras and sample audiences. In a
strange and eerie way, it is these training sessions, this
successful disciplining of an Austrian/German mouth on
which so much of modern history hinges – it is a black
hole still bending history in its disastrous direction.

The movie, *My Fair Lady*, provides another example of
the oral disciplining that any social ambitions and ascend
in society requires. The two protagonists, Eliza Doolittle
and Professor Henry Higgins, are the antagonistic
forces in the movie that find themselves fighting over
the same tongue, the same mouth. It is both a very
small and a very large space to conquer: as small as
Doolittle´s/Audrey Hepburn´s physical mouth – as vast
as the difference between high and low in English class
society. The schizophrenia of human reality is here
made abundantly clear: Doolittle is the personification
of matter, Higgins is the personification of concepts
and ideas. The former is hot, loud, spontaneous and
vulgare; the latter is cool, distant, controlled and refined.
Presence and representation, body and image, laughter
and language are here repeating and restaging their age-
old fight inside the terrorized voice and vocabulary of
Hepburn. As we know, logos will prove victorious in the

Anders Kølle
in conversation with images by Ashley YK Yeo

end. And it wins through a violent act of sculpting and
reshaping that must first disembody and objectify the
mouth, isolate it and numb it, in order to turn it, bit by bit,
syllable by syllable, into a pure and noiseless instrument
of English refinement and reason. To be sure, it is no
longer Doolittle´s mouth. It is a passage fully occupied
by impersonal forces, fully in the service of discourse and
reason. Doolittle herself is sent in orbit around this mouth
that now belongs to something else – something, to her,
alien and disturbing. To emerge as a perfect, articulate
butterfly she must sacrifice herself, she must lose herself
as a bodily, sensuous being. Logos, language and death
here form a perverse triangle in which the professor
sits like a giant spider, waiting for his perfect *Rain in
Spain* – which is to say: Professor Higgins is also a Dr.
Frankenstein who dismantles and dismembers in order to
create new, artificial and perfectly articulated life. Death
is the tunnel that the subject must through to be reborn
on the side of logos. Doolittle can do little about it.
Something has captured her mouth and she is not getting
it back. But in a fictional way this apparently strange
destiny of Doolittle only reflects a very real experience
that every child must go through: The disciplining of
the mouth that makes entry into society – especially its
better and more desirable circles – possible.

How to properly stage the mouth presents humanity
with unending problems. The forces that fight for this
little cave are constantly pulling it in different directions.
In good and polite company we must speak much and
eat little; in relaxed and informal company we must
eat much and speak little. It all depends on where the
accentuation should be, who or what the mouth should
serve and accommodate: body or logos? Pleasure or
reason? Silver cutlery and pizza trays, crystal glasses and
cardboard mugs, napkins and greasy fingers are but a

continuation of this rift and fault line through the human psyche. And in between, crossing back and forth are all kinds of objects and stage props, sometimes siding with reason, sometimes siding with pleasure: Lipstick aestheticizes speech and turns aesthetics verbal. It is the ornament hanging over the door to language. Cigarette smoke is both stressing the breath and blurring the mouth. It is a play and flirtation with rhythm and veiling. Moustaches and beards are gateways or forests, highways or bushes. They either overemphasize or obfuscate the origins of speech. Each individual must thus find his own solutions and negotiate his own peace. The mouth is always the center of too much attention. Dressed up or dressed down, painted or unpainted the conflicts it must solve and roles it must play are abundant: the lover´s mouth, the worker´s mouth, the sensuous mouth, the intelligent mouth, the happy mouth, the stern and commanding mouth – the mouths of mothers and fathers, of daughters and sons. Each mouth requires its own expressions – its own accentuations and proper manifestations. This complexity, however, can be boiled down to one single question on which all other questions and decisions hinges: is the mouth full or is it empty? Is it always already something or is it always only waiting to become something? Logos and pleasure, language and body provide very separate answers: to logos the mouth must at the outset be empty. It is a cave still waiting for its representations and cave paintings, that is: its language. If the mouth is not an empty space, language will have no place to occupy, speech no room to fill. Only as a void, then, can the mouth be the potential for speech. Meaning and signification, the very act of symbolization requires this darkroom to develop its pictures. It is in the secretive darkness of an unfilled space that the fullness of meaning is born. It is, by the way, in the very same manner that Freud

regards the female sex: like the mouth, the female sex
is for Freud a lack, a pure nothing, and it is around this
lack that the entire sexual economy rotates. Without
this void as the starting point – this zero from which all
fantasies as well as fears originates – sexuality would
have no space in which to project its pictures. The
female sex, then, mirrors the mouth as the economy
of sex mirrors the rules of language. Lacan has already
looked deeply into these mirrors and analyzed the many
intricate connections: the relations between language
and castration, between the Name-of-the-father and
the entry into speech. The possibility of language is thus
constantly related to cracks and voids and situated in
concealed darkness.

If logos must regard the mouth as empty, the body must
see the mouth as full – or, more precisely: to the body,
the mouth is neither empty nor full – the mouth simply is.
This is the simple presence of the mouth in a kiss. This is
the being of breath and of lips in a moment´s embrace:
the presence of flesh, of warmth, of respiration. The kiss
doesn´t fill the mouth since the mouth is not a void but
always already there, always already and undoubtedly
something. This is the presence that the kissers present
and give to each other: a being beyond discourse and
articulation. Surely, kisses can be practiced and steps
towards kisses rehearsed. All kinds of plans and strategies
be made – and kisses can be endlessly debated and
discussed both before and after the kiss. But the kiss
itself must return the schemers and planners to the
reality of an unplannable, unforeseeable now. The meeting
of lips exceeds and overflows discourse in all directions
and frees the mouth of its verbal and phonetic bonds.
Unlike language, unlike logos, it has no darkrooms in
which to develop its pictures since there are no distances
and secrets to be protected. Doolittle could do little

with logos but she was undoubtedly an excellent kisser –
whereas we can be pretty certain that Professor Higgins
was not. Disciplined mouths are bound to fail in the art of
kissing – they drag too much control across the doorstep
to immediate, bodily being. And yes, prudent and forced
kissers and kisses exist – they land on the foreheads of
awkwardly smiling children all the time. But such kisses
are bound to be laughable since they find themselves
hopelessly trapped between two forces of equal strength:
the body that requires spontaneity and presence and the
discourse that demands distance and control. In the end,
the prudent kiss becomes neither and lands unwillingly
in a laughable no-man´s-land. This, however, is the only
kind of kiss, the only dubious sign of feeling and affection
that people in power are allowed. The genuine kiss with
its transgressions of logos, with its immediacy and bodily
presence is a risk that power cannot take. It brings too
much light and too much surface into a room that needs
both its depths and its darkness to exist. The political
speech is therefore the "natural" home of the politician –
a space in which he feels protected and secure – whereas
the kiss is always accompanied by outlandish feelings, by
sudden stage fright and fear: how will it look this time?
Hopefully, better than last time.

And laughter? We already know on which side laughter
is placed. Laughter is the mouth that grows and grows
to reach the size of the mouth of an opera singer but
without any arias and words to spout out. Laughter has
the megalomania of a diva and yet none of her ambitions
and vanities. It is the manifestation of lack of discipline
par excellence and therefore also the strongest opponent
to power. In the film, *The Great Dictator* – in a beautiful
but deeply defiant gesture Chaplin turned the world
Hitler was burning into a floating, dancing balloon. While
Hitler drilled his mouth for speeches, Chaplin freed it

for laughter – indeed, a battle between caves and light, between darkrooms and bodily presence. The body that Hitler could only relate to as destined for combat and death, Chaplin would seek to emancipate from all such sinister claims and ideas. Like a reversed Professor Higgins he would move from discipline to freedom, from ideologies to matter, from discourse to being to return all the Eliza Doolittles of this world to their original, unmolested state. It is a battle over the mouth that keeps repeating itself. Discourse and body, language and presence are constantly on the lookout for speaking and laughing mouths. Most of us find ourselves working for both sides and constantly oscillating back and forth as dubious double agents of these superpowers. It is the great malleability of the mouth that makes such schizophrenic behavior possible. But wherever we may momentarily find ourselves, whatever speeches or kisses we may be engaged in and at whatever dinner-tables we are seated for a longer or a shorter while, we remain and are without interruptions and hesitations in the full service of the absurd.

One Return Ticket, Please

Traveler: *I would like one return ticket, please.*
Booking clerk: *Certainly. Where to?*
Traveler: *Here, of course.*

Laughter is a sort of return ticket. We always end up where we were. And where we have been in the meantime, what journey we have undertaken, remains unspeakable. As in the joke above, only the point of departure and the point of return are known and inscribe themselves in an order of calculable hours and on a map of definable locations. Nothing has changed and everything has changed. The departure and the return form their own little perfect circle. And yet, as Derrida has taught us, no return is every quite that simple and every attempt at a repetition always haunted by a difference – which is to say: even if the booking clerk in the joke knew what the traveler meant, he would still be in his right to ask: Where to?

The German philosopher, Ernst Bloch, once recounted this strange and thought-provoking Jewish parable: "A rabbi, a real cabalist, once said that in order to establish the reign of peace it is not necessary to destroy everything nor to begin a completely new world. It is sufficient to displace this cup or this brush or this stone just a little, and thereby everything. But this small displacement is so difficult to achieve and its measure so difficult to find that, with regard to the world, humans are incapable of it and it is necessary that the Messiah come."[7] In Judaism as well as in Christianity everything hinges on this Messianic return which is also the main cause of dispute, rupture, and conflict between the two religions: For has He already returned or is He yet to return? The return ticket is bought and paid for, everyone agrees, but the return itself is uncertain and haunted by *différance*: deferred or not deferred? Completed or

[7] Leland de la Durantaye, *Giorgio Agamben – A Critical Introduction* (Stanford: Stanford University Press, 2009), p. 380

Anders Kølle
in conversation with images by Ashley YK Yeo

yet to be completed? Without going to such Messianic lengths or any deeper into this Messianic return, we may, however, use the parable for our own profane purposes: For isn´t humor as well a question of small displacements: the displacement of a cup, a brush or a stone in a sketch – the displacement of a word, a meaning, an intention in a joke? To find something funny means to find something out of place and the usual order disturbed. It is a small difference, it is an unsuccessful encounter, an empty grasp in the air. To find something funny means, in other words, not to find it at all – and this very failure and disorientation is the source of much amusement and the (not)finder´s reward. Humor constantly revolves around misunderstandings and encounters that never take place – or which do, eventually, take place but neither at the location nor at the time expected. It is the return of a barred return, a return of disrupted relations: words and things no longer connect in their habitual way but move in unexpected directions. Not only habits are hereby questioned and momentarily disturbed but also the calculable world and world of calculability on which these habits are based: the rules of grammar, the rules of space and time, the rules of logos. Humor always entails some sort of unworking of systems, some kind of "désoeuvrement" of the functions and workings of everyday life. The effect of such short machine stops should not be underestimated. As the parable says: it is not necessary to destroy everything nor to begin a completely new world. It is enough with a small displacement.

Once again, the affinities between humor and art – their shared strategies in the unworking of our habitual world – are worth a short return: Art is, as humor, full of displacements as well as reorganizations that organize themselves around new and alien centers. When Picasso

displaces an eye, a nose, an ear – when he displaces
and disjoints a neck, a shoulder – he is evoking a return
that, however, does not return and a representation that
no longer re-presents in its usual sense. It is enough
to displace a female profile to make all women and
all of humanity look, if just for a moment, eerily and
exceedingly strange. And the fact that this displaced
eye or nose is not the result of an error, that it cannot
be explained or excused as an accident, makes the
displacement significant without, however, revealing in
what direction and to what end it now signifies instead. It
is as if the poles of the world have moved ever so slightly,
as if some unknown forces of gravitation are pulling the
human figure in an odd and unforeseeable direction.
Picasso is not the destroyer of faces and bodies nor
does he paint a completely new world. All that he does
– and this is surely a lot – is to hand us a return ticket to
the female face that, however, only leads to delays and
deferrals. Somehow, somewhere he and we get lost on
the way and it is this loss of orientation, this loss of a
return, that is the (not)finder´s artistic reward. It is just
as strange and ridiculous as it sounds: Picasso´s artistic
genius lies entirely in him being a terrible tour guide. He
is the master of misencounters and broken promises – or,
more precisely: what he promises is precisely to break his
promise. In this sense, he shares more with comedians
than he would probably like and acknowledge: the only
promise of a walking comedian is that he must stumble
and fall; the only promise of a balancing comedian
is that he must lose his balance. It is constantly the
unexpected we expect, the unanticipated we anticipate.
Modern art and comedy evoke the exact same appetite
for displacements and surprises. When Cubism became
a style and a school – when the displacements were no
longer "wrong" but "right" and entirely expected – was
also the moment when these same displacements lost

Anders Kølle
in conversation with images by Ashley YK Yeo

their artistic and critical potential – the moment when the museum ticket booths returned to selling their usual return tickets. In the end, the comedian who balances and doesn´t fall might be funnier than the one who does.

If great comedians like great artists are in love with their own mishaps and slippages it is not because these slippages and mishaps offer them an entirely new world but because they offer them the very same world, our world, once again. It is a repetition bound to go wrong, it is a repetition that, of course, is never successful and from this failure reality makes its limping return. One must be open to the possibility that great abstractionist painters like great comedians make all their tremendous efforts and all their strange and illogical detours because they are deeply in love with reality and love the world exactly as it is. In a sense, they are no less realists than the painters who strive to repeat every detail as precisely as possible and who thereby end up creating perfect fictions of perfect but impossible returns. But this reality that they love, this kind of realism that they seek is, however, no longer a reality compatible with logos. It is a reality that goes beyond the rules of logos, the rules of good and common sense, to explore a larger and expanded reality beyond the scope and control of human reason. It is a realism that is bound to appear unrealistic, sometimes even provocatively strange, when regarded from the perspective of habitual meanings. It is also, therefore, a realism that is often deemed childish and amateurish since it is measured according to standards and weighed on scales of the habitual world – scales that finds flaws and imbalances wherever its own fictional world is not perfectly and unambiguously repeated. It is the same reality and a very different one. It is a perfect return that goes perfectly wrong. But if asked where to the return ticket should go the answer would be an unhesitant: here.

It is always the smallest, most narrow, definition of reality that so-called "realists" subscribe to. The real needs to be small because it needs to be governable. And in order to be governable it must be logical and one-sided – that is: expressible in either numbers, formulas or words. God doesn´t play dice with the universe, as Einstein famously said. But, surely, this is not God speaking but human, fallible reason. Indeed, God may turn out to be a greater and more passionate gambler than Einstein and his fellow "realists" were ready to accept. That is why Heisenberg´s uncertainty principle and Niels Bohr´s principle of complementarity present the sciences with such unending problems. It seems to force a one-way ticket on modern physics without offering any hope of a speedy return. The safety of representation, of a world that offers and surrenders itself to our human mirroring and reason, is thoroughly undermined by an ambiguous and unstable underworld of immeasurable and unpredictable movements. It is statistics instead of certainties, it is a portrait of the world in which it is always up for debate where the eye, the nose, the ear should be. What "looks" most like reality? Particles or waves? They both look right in their own way. Physics looks down into an abyss in which their models start to resemble something quite unacceptable for these most sober and cool-headed men and women: they begin to look like art. Instead of one picture of reality there are many. Each faction and school develops its own style, its own particular representations. Physics is a canvas that is constantly being reworked and covered in new layers of paint. It still desires just one picture, just one single answer, but in the process it creates so many. A little anecdote to illustrate the point: When Einstein was celebrated as one of Germany´s greatest geniuses of all times, he modestly replied that he was in no way a genius comparable to Beethoven, since while Beethoven had created something new, he,

on the other hand, had never done anything but describe
what was already there. Creativity and logos, art and
science, are, thus, once more placed in opposition: the
former makes, the latter mirrors – the one moves away
from the world, the other simply returns. It all depends
on whether one has bought a one-way ticket or a return
ticket in God´s grand ticket booth. And, surely, Einstein´s
personal humbleness and modesty only reflects the
immodesty and megalomania of his profession: the true
representation of the world belongs to science. Artists
can do whatever they want and it may be very beautiful
and quite amusing, but in matters of truth, of real returns
to reality, only science stands a chance.

A scientist that laughs is a mad scientist. Comic books,
adventure movies and sci-fi movies are full of laughing
professors. These men are all brilliant but their brilliance
is touched by something eerie, something strange
that continuously threatens their masterful logics and
impeccable reason to turn disastrous illogical and break
completely down. It is the portrait of a science that
exceeds itself, that overflows its own borders, and thereby
reaches domains in which it is bound to get lost. The mad
professor is a prophetic seer and a blind man at one and
the same time: he always sees too much, he continuously
sees too far ahead, and this peculiar and immodest seeing
turns him blind to his own transgressions and trespassing.
On the way to new inventions and brilliant creations,
he unwillingly and unknowingly oversteps his limits. His
laughter is the very symbol of this overstepping. His
laughter irrupts precisely at the point where the limits
of logos are transgressed. This is not a laughter that is
shared by others, not a joyful and contagious laughter,
but a lonely and isolated laughter since it is the result
of his very singular and isolated journey. The eerie and
ominous quality of this laughter stands in direct relation

to its isolation: to laugh on one´s own means to be alone with the absurd – it means to see and encounter the absurd where nobody else is either able or willing to find it. The mad professor is thus a tragic figure and his lonely destiny is sealed from the beginning: his entire trajectory is closely followed and eventually overtaken by destruction and death. We, as audiences, hardly pity him since the entire narrative has positioned us against him, placing us unequivocally on the safe and healthy side of good and common reason. Madness and laughter only appear as flirtations with the absurd, as transgressions that may tickle our curiosity and satisfy our appetite for the strange and uncommon, but that, in the end, are called back and annulled. Once again, it comes down to the kind of ticket one has bought: a one-way ticket or a return ticket? And then, again, what one means by a return ticket? To what world, to what reality? It is, of course, entirely possible to go against the stream and side with the mad professor. In that case, the whole order and logic of the story is also displaced. It is, as in the Jewish parable, the small displacement that brings about much greater changes. First of all, it would invite us to think that the mad professor is, in fact, not mad but only the discoverer and revealer of hidden secrets: that science too has its limits and its outer borders; that science too stands in connection with the absurd. Perhaps, one might then join the professor and create an entire choir of laughs that laughs both with and against humanity and all of our human efforts to keep the absurd at bay. Wouldn´t this also be a sort of return?

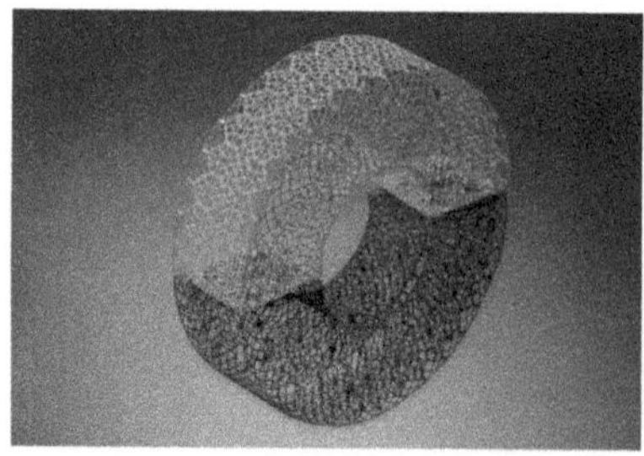

A Space Between Those Spaces, 2020
Hand-cut Paper
9 × 18 × 5.2 cm (Papercut Sculpture)
122 × 40 × 40 cm (Installation)

Pale Violet, 2020
Hand-cut Paper with Pigment
1.5 × 13 × 28.5 cm (Papercut Sculpture)
110.5 × 42 × 27 cm (Installation)

Drop of Light (Pyramid), 2019
Hand-cut Paper
6.7 × 6.7 × 15 cm

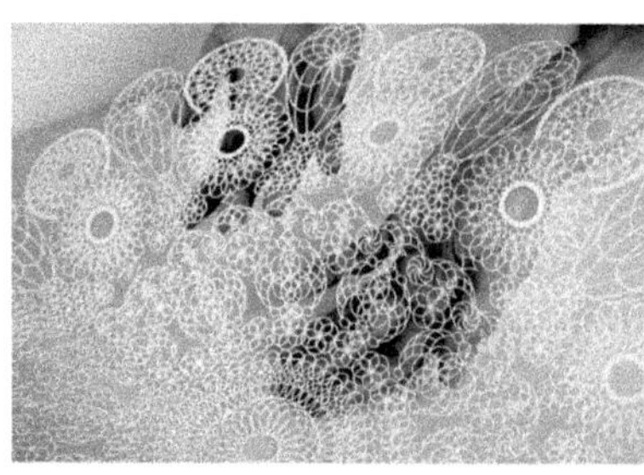

A Soft Spring, 2020
Hand-cut Paper
44.5 × 4 4.5 cm (Papercut Sculpture)
62.8 × 62.8 × 4.9 cm (Framed)

Angels Lips, 2023
Hand-cut Paper, Mica, Pigment
8 x 8 x 13.5 cm (Papercut Sculpture)

Poetics of Paper

The Singaporean artist, Ashley YK Yeo, seems in every possible way out of sync with our time, going up against the collective stream of developments, fashions and tendencies that characterize our present moment: her work is delicate in a time of brutality, her work is slow in a time of massive acceleration, her work is handmade in a time of digitalization, her work is diminutive and reserved in a time of loud effects and of boastful, self-promoting expressions. Her work is, in other words, hopelessly out of touch with the small, unimaginative field that we like to call "reality"; and from this hopelessness, from this strange exile of hers she returns with a paper pearl, she emerges with her fragile paper sculptures and places them before us as signs and letters of a forgotten language — a gesture that would appear naïve, ridiculous even, if it wasn´t so serious, so sincere and so pregnant with poetical reflections and poetical defiance. Over the years she has carefully chosen and perfected the expressive weapons that she now turns against the ills of our time: paper against plastic, arabesques against alienation, presence and contemplative attendance against the superficial and hasty encounters of social life today.

It is a simple, yet significant fact that all her sculptures are handmade, each motif and pattern carefully brought to the fore through a meticulous delineation and selection of cuts. The hand, the paper, the scissor constitute a dynamic triangle in which something hitherto unthinkable becomes perceptible and thinkable for the first time. It is a space of encounters between potentiality and actuality, a balancing act between what is and what could be, between visions and envisions, traversing a field of possibilities as thin as a paper but as deep as an artist´s imagination. In the end a sculpture emerges, a work manifests itself, becomes concrete. But this concretization has a peculiar quality in Yeo´s work.

Fragile as it is, constituted of a myriad of tiny punctures
and holes, her work doesn´t stand forth with the self-
assuredness of a work that securely belongs to this world,
a work that has now emerged to claim its rightful place
and the public´s admiration and applause, but rather as
a hesitant birth, a coming into being that lingers, steps
back and forth on a ghostly threshold, neither belonging
fully to this world nor truly locatable in another. Like an
infant still unsure about its own role and about its proper,
physical dimensions it emerges and retreats indecisively
before us. Hence it is up to us, the audience, to lure it into
this world, to call it into being, to encourage it to take
the final step into material and perceptual existence — a
process that can only be successful, if we, the audience,
call, lure and encourages in the right way: that is, by
devoting ourselves fully to the contemplation of the
work. There is no middle way, no flimsy attention, no
hasty and superficial perception that will achieve this.
One has to move close, both in physical and in attentive,
phenomenological terms in order to see it. Thus the
second peculiar fact about Yeo´s art: her works are
small — so small, in fact, that one may very easily miss
them. Full of details, as they are, they themselves are
not much more than white, snowflake-like details in a
world of large and colorful things that constantly call
for attention. Her work therefore asks something that
many of us, easily distracted citizens of the modern
world, almost have forgotten how to give — something
that we must now rediscover or re-invent in front of her
oeuvre: the meaning of intimacy, the value of integrity,
of uncompromised and uncompromising attention. To
see her work one must leave one world behind in order
to gain another. This is how unwavering Yeo is, how
demanding she is and what she whispers to the attentive
ear with her voice of sculpted paper.

Anders Kølle is lecturer of Communication Arts at Khon Kaen
University, Thailand. Holding a PhD in Media and Communications
from The European Graduate School, he has taught art and
philosophy at several universities, including the University of
Copenhagen and Assumption University, Bangkok.

His work focuses on contemporary encounters between
philosophy and art, and on art´s potential to produce new modes
of thinking and create new forms of critique.

His publications include *The Technological Sublime* (Singapore:
Delere Press, 2018), and *Beyond Reflection* (New York: Atropos
Press, 2013).

Encompassing drawings and art objects, **Ashley YK Yeo**'s practice stems from private thoughts and ontological questioning. She is currently interested in maintaining a relationship with nature. Her practice revolves around themes of lightness and slowness.

Ashley completed her Master´s Degree in Fine Arts at Chelsea College of Art & Design, London. She attained her BA (Hons) from LASALLE College of Arts, Singapore with first class honors.

She has been shortlisted for the LOEWE Craft Prize (2018).